LOVEINABOOKSTOREORYOURMONEYBACK
SARAH QUIGLEY

LOVEINABOOKSTOREORYOURMONEYBACK
SARAH QUIGLEY

AUCKLAND UNIVERSITY PRESS

for Rachel

First published 2003

Auckland University Press
University of Auckland
Private Bag 92019
Auckland
New Zealand
http://www.auckland.ac.nz/aup

© Sarah Quigley, 2003

ISBN 1 86940 284 7

National Library of New Zealand Cataloguing-in-Publication Data
Quigley, Sarah.
Love in a bookstore or your money back / Sarah Quigley.
ISBN 1-86940-284-7
1. Love poetry, New Zealand. 2. Authors—Poetry. I. Title.
NZ821.2—dc 21

Publication is assisted by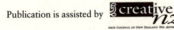

This book is copyright. Apart from fair dealing for the purpose of private study, research, criticism or review, as permitted under the Copyright Act, no part may be reproduced by any process without prior permission of the publisher.

Cover design: Neil Pardington, Eyework Design

Printed by Publishing Press Ltd, Auckland

Contents

Love, or

On coming back from *The Big Lebowski*   2
Science or chemistry   3
After midnight is a missing   4
Bridal   5
Sebastian, six months on   6
Making sushi in the afternoon with my sister   7
meeting nino   8
Orari   9
Her white fingers   10
In the soundshell   11
Lufthansa 457 to Frankfurt   12
Santa Maria de Feira   13
Age-old   15
December   16

money back?

Gallery   18
The Kapinos Equation   19
A green china squirrel in a shop window   21
Dinosaur Times   22
The big woman and the tiny woman   24
Catching up with family   25
Infidelity, of a kind   27
biodegradable   28

On receiving bad news at the Adelphi Motel   29
arriving yourself   30
Floating in the astronaut hour   31
The radiologist   33
Weather reports on the kitchen table late at night   34
The pomegranate is seductive   35
Restless   36
Running low   37
Sensation White   38

The bookstore

New York Four   40
How the world goes on   44
The writer   45
The Haiku Master is dead   47
She sang 'green green' and moved to blue   48
Reading at the Daadgalerie   49
Poetry is the hardest thing   50
Poem for Anna   51
The *mot juste*   52
For Joe, on a Monday afternoon   54
Love in a bookstore or your money back   55

LOVE, OR

On coming back from *The Big Lebowski*

If I could have written a book
just like this film
I would have done so.

Dream sequences deserts pornographic
queens white suits and white russians,
and a sense of humour deeper than
the cowboy's voice which sends us out
into the night saying

sam elliott.

If I could have written a film
I would have done so,
but would I have written you in
beside me?

This is harder than the million dollar
ransom drop off the side of a wooden bridge

harder than the baseball bat
which cracked Jeff Bridges' answer
phone like an egg

sunny side up?
but it is dark when we come out,
and rain is flying,

and it is too hard to write,
it is more than hard
to right real life

make more than
creative choices.

Science or chemistry

Your voice on the phone
gives a jumpstart
to my heart.

Is this a cliché?
Perhaps.

But because you are
a scientist you will understand
when I say

it is also
a fact.

After midnight is a missing

He calls at midnight,
tells truths.

For instance:

– he would rather have a tin
of excellent Italian tomatoes than some
tasteless hothouse real ones

and a good can of watermelon juice
is superior to an indifferent melon.

– Many women look better
after crying (their faces have
a washed-clean look) and

men are nothing more than lapdogs.

– You should take a leaf from the Japanese book,
shed your shoes at the door.

*

Afterwards, walk around in socks
and listen to the line
ringing with absence,

carry the phone to the window,
watch wires loop away over the dark city,
know only two things with certainty:

– silence is not always golden

– after midnight is a kind of missing.

Bridal

The cork trees that day
turned their faces politely away,
linking soft arms
over our heads.

Pollen fell like small pieces
of rain.

And for that hour we,
who had held our breath
for most of our shared life,
were not afraid to fall.

Sebastian, six months on

You fell out of an airmail
envelope with the rustle of
wind in a palm tree,

a tiny breath of Wellington
winter in the middle of that
San Diego summer.

For six months you sat
in the shape of a small square
birth notice on my fridge.

When we met, you already
knew how to hold the attention
of a coffee table, already held

the sky in your eyes. You
threw spoons on the ground
with determination and grabbed

my heart.

Making sushi in the afternoon with my sister

I have never made sushi, although
I have eaten it in London
and LA

but tomorrow
at 5.30 in the afternoon
I will be making sushi with my sister.

At 5.30 my sister will arrive in her white car
with wasabi, rice vinegar
and know-how

and next thing you know
there will be elegant food for the masses,
or food for the elegant masses, or both –

tomorrow, in the late afternoon.
This is what can happen when you have a sister.

Later, many hours after 5.30, friends will roll
out of my house wrapped around seaweed
wrapped around rice

by your clever fingers,
and I will still not know how to make sushi.
(Sushi-making is not necessarily in the genes.)

But when glasses lie on their sides
and the street lamps look away from the window,
I will know what I can do when you are with me

when you are here.

meeting nino

he emerges slowly
into a room he doesn't know,

head thrown back,
throat exposed,
skin a little grainy
from travelling long distances.

even so, he's smiling.

he has been sent by you,
is part of you, and so

i hold him carefully
in my hands so as not
to crease him.

this is nino, arriving by fax.

Orari

Shadow of a passing truck
silver and black
textured with pine needles

sliding as far as the window
and beyond.

A flea bite on my thigh
itching like a list of things to do

your arm hot and heavy over me

your muscles jumping again
through the day past

your mouth moving in my hair
like wind in a shelter belt

calling down sleep with the words
Orari Orari.

Her white fingers

It was the colours that were the important thing,
or so he thought as he sat
in the yellow room
on the blonde wood chair
and looked across at her white fingers.

Her white fingers
crossing like bird's legs,
wading in the pale blue china bowl,
folding the brown recycled paper napkin.

There is a grain of rice stuck between her two front teeth
and he loves her –

God, how he loves her.

The water grows milky from the residue of rice
left on her light skin
(chopsticks are of the clearest beige).

The rind of the aubergine is so dark
that it looks like soil
recently cut by a spade.

As for the green of the pepper –
so light,
so bright!
It almost makes him cry.

In the soundshell

The wind's lips have blown
it like an egg and moved on. We
are held in white emptiness.

My stillness balances yours.
We sit lightly in each
other's head; only our eyes move.

It is so quiet I can hear
the beginning of your life. This is
the place between the audible minutes.

We exist within paper
walls. When you leave,
tread carefully.

Lufthansa 457 to Frankfurt

His feet are propped against
the wall, expensive shiny loafers
with flat and shiny soles.

They might have walked down
long Italian streets, those shoes,
but they have never stepped over
a sea of lawn to you.

He asks for newspapers,
scans the business pages
in three different European languages
and checks his stocks and shares,

he appears to be satisfied by what he reads,
that man, but he doesn't know his losses
because he's never talked about the sound of poetry
with you.

And when his head lies back and he looks at me
there are several recent continents in his eyes,
but they are tired of the world
and because of this I know one thing without a doubt:
they have never looked at you.

Santa Maria de Feira

Driving at last through a tollgate,
past the white dome of a convention centre,
they made their way into a hot and tired town
tied about with motorways and slumped
at the bottom of a valley.

There they stopped the car.
On foot, they entered a cobbled square
where everything was blank and shuttered
for this was a Saturday afternoon
in a country which still observed siesta hours.

Walking at last through the open doorway
of a dark and dusty shop that stocked lemonade
brought into that valley some years earlier

they paid their money, drank, lit cigarettes,
and turned expecting to see only
the dishevelled, exhausted,
the frayed and impossible sky:

and they noticed instead a wedding party
riding out of the church door opposite
on the long tongue of a red carpet.

The bright bride sailed down the steps
towards the next day, and all the days
to follow were carried behind
by the solemn, irrepressible groom!

Seeing at last that their own immediate
past would fade – the roadside stop, the smeared
and empty sandwich cabinets, the shop-girl
walking on curled disconsolate toenails
towards the cash register –

believing this they, too, emerged
into the heat and felt its breath
as an affirmation on their faces:
that is, it no longer smelt of despair,
and they heard song in the hot trees.

Age-old

'You have a big head,'
said the sun conversationally,
'and a big heart for
someone who is only two.'

'My prediction for you – '
(said the sun, in a casual kind of way)

but already the baby had closed
his eyes, shutting them down
like cool venetians

for although he was only
two-years wise he knew that the sun
could, occasionally, be unreliable

and also that it was easier to grow
undazzled by other people's
expectations.

December

You arrived in the night
        quietly like the snow.

When I looked out
        the houses had been picked up
and put back down in a different
place.

Stairways were made beautiful.

The trees sang
        in small white voices,
people smiled.

MONEY BACK?

Gallery

Olivia talks of escape
while over her shoulder
monster faces stare.

Their pupils reveal recent contact
with a photographer but each incidental touch
sets them quivering.

Olivia talks of *escape*
under gallery light as deathly as mountains;
the light on the photographed stubble of the faces
is as sharp as a razor.

From the opposite wall the German Senate frown,
fingerprints smearing their glass shoulders.
Smoke hangs flag-like in the air,
metal frames suspended above bent necks.

All calmness is manufactured here.

And – 'All the pupils are blue,'
says the gallerist

but the concrete floor strikes upwards
like a snake,
and Olivia talks of escape

while outside trams are hurling
towards the final hour.

The Kapinos Equation

(for Micha Kapinos)

He was a big man but he hunched
all of his six feet under the table
when speaking of his arrival
at the barracks of the 3rd Division

around noon in 1979
where soon he would begin sixteen-hour days
alongside a fleshy butcher from East Germany

making meatballs for three thousand
in pans recently vacated by rats.

(Outside the steaming windows
the Warsaw Pact was collapsing
and there were faces in the flying mud

and the occasional night was spent
in a metal car in the middle of a forest because
Russia had decided to invade Afghanistan.)

Once, on answering *no* three times
to the question 'Have you done machine guns,
shooting, or hand grenades?' he was taken away
from his hotplate into a dual landscape of snow and sand

where, passing an officer with a face on fire,
he was ushered into an enclosure and handed
one small metallic object which he proceeded to throw
straight and hard through the middle of the shouts
and instructions, and the general panic.

Then he walked on out of there
to begin ten more months of cooking from
oh six hundred to twenty-two o'clock

for, although at the age of sixteen
he had been an Olympic high jumper
and had soared above the bar,

he was equally skilled at keeping his head
down when he knew better.

A green china squirrel in a shop window,

well, it says all that needs to be said,
that small china squirrel sitting
in the window over there.

Its stomach holds the clear
green swell of an afternoon
too full of itself to rely on.

The hunch of its head, its chipped
immobile ears, tell us everything
about when, and where:

for instance, it is late in the year,

the light is heading for the hills,
it is a time for hoarding,
there is hunger in the air.

Dinosaur Times

You have brought me closer
to extinction than I have ever been
in the whole of my middle-sized life.

You, who were not even extraordinary!
With your round-toed shoes,
your polite well-modulated voice,

and your way of sometimes using
the word *quiet* instead of *quite*,
after which you would bite your lip.

You led me to the very edge
of a ravine on a day so cold that
breathing felt like a payback
for some kind of happiness.

Together we looked down
on road markers of mist
and the grey metallic fingernails of the gulls –
a sight seen more often from below.

And although my lungs hurt
you made me stay and look down further
still to where a desert lay,
scattered with white chalky remains.

Once I had acknowledged the bottom
of the world, you pointed out how far away
from it we were, and how close the sky was
to our faces on that particular day.

If you climbed on my shoulders,
you said, *I expect you could touch it.*

Then, after we had stood for quite some time
where no one (we believed) had ever stood before,
you took yourself away: neatly,
surgically, with the greatest of skill.
You, who were not even extraordinary!

After your removal I lay quiet
among the bones, listening to the birds cry.
Each day had the potential
to become an age.

And I would say this to you now:
if it were not for my constant vigilance
over the state of my heart,
if not for the hard-won years
stacked at my back like a wall to lean on
in times of fright

– well, let's just say that
for the first time and because of you,
there was nearly no more of me.

The big woman and the tiny woman

She has the big woman's thing
about tiny women

at least that's what the rest of the room
has been told before the entrance
of the tiny woman
who sits now on the floor, in front of
the big woman.

She – that is, the big woman –
sits on the sofa tilting towards
her millionaire man

and presses her large red mouth
to his with huge
intensity

while the tiny woman sits on the floor
politely sipping punch.
She wonders what to say when
the red mouth comes off
the rich one?

You see, she – that is, the tiny woman –
has the single woman's fear
of the married woman.

Catching up with family

The three girls stand wearing
ponchos in varying shades of brown
that their uncle has brought them back
from Peru.

(one of them is four)

They stand in varying brown poses
against a faded brown fence made from
long pieces of photographed wood.

(one of them is a heart surgeon)

Their faces are screwed up against
the sun in varying attitudes of decay against
a burnt-out fence criss-crossed with long shade.

(one of them has survived skin cancer)

The tallest one has flung her Peruvian hand
over the knitted neck and shoulders
of the smallest.

(all of them could be under six)

They are lit by fringes of llama wool
that has been brought long distances
from the glaring white slopes of the Andes.

(their uncle has since been caught in an avalanche)

They stand on the kitchen window sill
in a surprising state of symmetry
brought about by a trick of photography.

(one of them might possibly be dead)

faces screwed up against the sun
dial

backs to the defensive
fence

eyes wired open
to stare down

time.

Infidelity, of a kind

I've been dreaming about you
the whole night long, I said

(this is what I said
after morning came, after
I came, after orgasm).

The truth was,
I had only dreamt of you once.

The rest of the time
it had been other men
parading through our black bedroom

walking in one side of my head
and out the other
leaving behind residual lust
and the dust of many more
and far greater orgasms
than the one I'd just had.

Heading for the front door,
those men,
before morning came along

and they got their arses kicked
by consciousness.

biodegradable

the walls of your life
are getting thinner

soon, they will fold in
on each other

one
one
one
one

and you will be ready
for recycling

On receiving bad news at the Adelphi Motel

Wet jasmine, and she has the feeling
that her heart has fallen down
and won't be getting up in a hurry.

Lawn made of astroturf is hidden
under water, travesty of its lime-green self
(travesty in itself) and she is watching

a heavy woman in a dark blue hat
walking up the drive with a stride
like thunder. There is a cake tin

in the woman's hands – *why?* – there is
a cake tin in her hands, and the ricochet rain
is hammering on the jubilee lid.

The newspaper sky rips overhead,
her eyes are disintegrating but still she is blindly
certain that the thunderous woman

will always
be walking
with the tin.

She never would have guessed it,
she has known it forever,
like the same-old saying

and the band plays on.

Same rain, same band,
the tin, the rain and the band

and

and –

you see? Already she is settling
into the long stride of grief.

arriving yourself

when you arrive

well, little to do
except wait for some
kind of settling

nothing to do but
take off your fake
fur coat in thirty-two
degree heat

while a one-minute
person with a good heart
stops your suitcase
from being wheeled away

little to do but go
to bed, lie back and
listen to the weather

(hail on the skylight
a welcome violence
that could be mistaken
for happiness)

nothing else for it but
turn your head on the pillow
looking for familiarity

which appears at two
windows wearing
two different faces

and is unfamiliar in both.

Floating in the astronaut hour

Suddenly the future
was nowhere to be seen.
On long pale legs it had run
out of the room
and into the street

so that in a matter of minutes
it had disappeared.

While you were bent
over the present, fully absorbed,
yes while you had been giving your *full attention* to:

a man,
a woman,
a job,
or the lyrics of a particularly beautiful and evasive song

yes, while you had been so busy there
bending inside the closed room –
while you had been so busy and so grave,
intent on identifying what was right in front of you,

the future had simply picked itself up,
packed itself up, and run silently away
leaving no echoes behind

and only the faintest sense of ever having been there,
nothing more than air which might not
have settled back
into place.

Once you realised this your sense of unease was profound
and you also rushed outside
onto the high balcony.

Five floors below you the trafficking street;
but you craned down and out,
hoping for some glimpse of the running months ahead,
for some reminder of what it was to be connected

(the scorch of the hand rail, the slice of a tile
on the bloodied underside of a toe,
a reminder of what it was to anticipate
pain, or a healing).

But above you the sky was crossed
like a donkey's back
and the distant scream of the trams below
had nothing to do with you.

Because of your earlier, some would say
your *excessive* attention to detail –
yes, because of your carelessness
or your over-care
now here you were
floating in the astronaut hour

which is what most people dream of
not realising (unless at some stage
the future has flung itself away from them too)
that too much space
is infinitely more disturbing
than too little.

The radiologist

Are you okay?, he says
and *You know I'm going to hurt
you*. He is so nice to you that a tear
falls from the side of your eye.

No one uses fountain pens
anymore but he has six grandchildren,
so he's allowed to leak ink into your veins
ready to read you over the weekend

and it's not an anachronism. You lie
watching the paper towel dispenser, watch
metal move gravely over you like the moon
over several nights and days.

He doesn't tell you anything
and you don't want to know. You lie flat
on a flat table, would like to protect yourself
with apron strings of lead,

want nothing to do with the long
corridor waiting outside, want never to be
delivered out of professional hands
into your own again.

Weather reports on the kitchen table late at night

The newspaper says
that it is two degrees in Oslo:
sunny, but close to freezing.

The isobars say
it will only be getting colder there,
where you are.

There, or in Helsinki
where you also occasionally work,
and where there will be snow
before tomorrow comes.

And I will be glad to think of you,
chapped hands in pockets,
eyes tight closed against the repeated
slaps of the wind,

cold and getting colder.

The truth of it is I would like you to feel
as cold as I felt when hearing
your voice at the end of a flat
uncomprehending phoneline

the last time,
for the last time.

The pomegranate is seductive

It's redder than your tongue

It wants you to touch it

It asks you to open it

with your mouth

Inside it's full of

semen-coloured cheese

It's running with watery juice

It's stuffed with seeds as hard as teeth

The pomegranate is a shattering disappointment

Restless

The light falls hard tonight
like a blow on the back of the neck
making it hard to remember people's names
when you come to say goodbye

and set off across the empty green field.
The wind always waits for you there.

Outside the cars have sucked the streets dry
and still all the way to go home
weaving your way through a world
of patio furniture and bad hair cuts.

You are being squeezed
in the angle of these streets.

The need to move on is growing
at the base of your spine
like a tumour,
only a matter of time

before you spit the stale air,
cut on out of there.

You are everyman,
nomad.

Running low

Watch me shrink as I run
along the waterfront,

arms, legs, nothing more,
feet falling after a rise
to meet the flat undramatic pavement.

The more I think
the more I am diminished,
would be twenty people,
can be only one
and do this one thing only –

running, low.

Keep arms prescribing angles
in the dull air,
move feet towards a crowd
that might or might not be watching,

and always with the knowledge that there is
a Swedish singer
a Russian actress
Greta Garbo or
Marlene Dietrich

waiting in the wings
larger than any one life, or twenty,

waiting for me to dwindle
to an insignificant point, at which time they will stroll
back in to you.

Sensation White

There is a time when the sky above you
is so huge that, should you throw a stone
high above your head, you might never
see that stone again:

a time when the horizon has become so hard
and bright that you are afraid to glance
that way in case you lose your sight:

a time when, searching for the ground,
you see only your own reflected legs
stretching to infinity so
it is no longer possible to walk.

This is a sensation often referred to
as grief. I call it a waiting time

or, simply, white.

THE BOOKSTORE

New York Four

I

And all the books at Barnes and Noble
have jagged edges
reminding you of where they came from

(cut from the arms of dried
and yellow American states
that you will never see).

And the lack of sleep suddenly
falls heavy on your shoulders
like a yoke so that

as you climb to the second floor
your feet kick the steps.

A shop full of wood and strangers;
and outside Soho
littering into the evening.

No one to talk to
until you find Frank O'Hara,
fall into his words
with relief and a catch in your throat
like a sob,
like a flaw in paper

because he first knew what it was
to be Manhattan-raw,
for the streets to flick you
like a finger, bent and released,
oblivious to you
and your personal history

which tonight has slipped
through your fingers like
a subway ticket into a drain.

Outside the streets are running
with people,
panic slides into anger
with a punch and the rain starts.

Shelter in a doorway smelling of piss and paint,
under your boots are sandwich crusts:
your only foothold in the whole of
this dark and roaring New York city.

II

Running fast down
Manhattan's East Side
and not so fast
down the West

past the foxy black girls
in their three-quarter pants
with flowers in their hair.

It's a foxy fast black Sunday in the Village,
and the heat is rising.

In the meat-packing district
there's blood on the walls,
piss on the cobblestones
and vomit in every doorway

but the Statue of Liberty
stands firm
and the clouds clear away after a week of rain.

Five-dollar palm readers put their feet up
on folding tables
and croon.

Round the bottom of the island
up past the fishmarkets
middle of the morning and the vendors long
gone

leaving shining scales in the air.

III

Anger at the turnstile
      of Broadway and Lafayette.
The ticket-seller's voice is magnified
and booms across the platform
to clash head-on with the oncoming train.

well fuck you asshole!

His angry legs and arms
      are cramped into a glass box
in a trick of the world,

carved in half daily
between his hot home country
and New York in July.

Too many Julys and
repeated humidity have made him sick
for home

so that all he can say are the magnified words

fuck you asshole

I am a nice person!

and still not able to hear his own defence.

IV

She sits in the dark blue chair
with the staple marks in the arms
retrieved from a pile of junk on Henry Street
which slips all the way down
to the Hudson River.

There she sits,
faint sweatmarks under her arms
and a sweat on her lip,

and around her head the wings
of resentment.

She is cornered, cornered,
but she *will not learn*,

with her dark blue silence
wills others not to leave.
Tension shines on her high cheekbones.

Outside a riot
or a basketball game in the street,

inside a sometime Madonna,
child feverish in the net cot,
fruit flies humming in the hot bananas.

How the world goes on

Running out of newspaper
and not ready to leave breakfast

I turn to poetry,

remember Primo Levi
and the pigeons purring all summer.

When I look outside
the sky is already purple,
the tree is lit.

Cars stream through the snow.

The writer

She sat for a long time
looking at the riddle of her next book.

The night went on,
footsteps went past the door,
the door banged.

She sat for a long time
looking at the riddle of
her next book:

– a quotation
– a clipping from a newspaper
– and something about someone
she had once known.

This was all she had been given.

The door to the courtyard banged,
the clock banged on into the night.
She sat for a lengthy, a looking time,
knowing no one but she
could solve it

and in so doing she became
the clock, the night,
the closing doors,
the words on the page
and the white hush between the words.

Knowing no one but she could solve it
brought with it a certain resolution,
as hard and pale as the night city:

and like the city she would wait
for the slow turning of time
to take hold
of the riddled ground,

to stretch its long arms
through the vacant riddled streets
and so in this long and waiting way
map out an answer.

The Haiku Master is dead

(in memory of Kinichi Sawaki)

The haiku master is dead.

Brevity in a box
where once it
grew serene

stretched its arms
to the limitless
white sky

opened its mouth

drank rain.

She sang 'green green' and moved to blue

'Green green,' she sang

and sang it, on and on,
until suddenly all the green came leaking out of the grass
and the bushes gave up on her, becoming
shadows of their former selves

and after that there was no more green
in the whole of her whole wide world.

She moved to blue.

'Blue blue!' she cried, and almost immediately
colour fell from the sky,
dropping in sheets around her
until she was drenched in blue.

But after a while the sun
dried that colour away
leaving her as pale and white
as she had ever been before.

'Brown?' she called, in an imperative voice,
and sure enough brown leapt from the trunks of the trees,
running low over the bleached grass
like a body of small moving animals.
Once it reached the horizon it paused,
just for a minute, and then was gone.

After that what was left for her to do?
Nothing but sit and stare at her own commanding
hands – the only thing left to her,

for she had not yet learnt to mix her colours
that they might last longer.

Reading at the Daadgalerie

Chinese and German,
neither my language;
two people speaking

page after page
of poetry –
my language.

See how the overhead
projector shimmers
with hidden meaning,

see the hot words
hang in the air
like exotic blossoms

quite quite beautiful
but not
quite

Poetry is the hardest thing

I

Not knowing how poetry went any more
or even if I'd ever had it
I went out to get drunk.

Vodka sharpens the mind
like a pencil.

Looking around for words
is like following garage sale signs
the day after.
Everything's already
in other people's houses.

II

I don't feel too good today.
Poetry pouring out of me
like a wound, won't dry up.

I remember words
and a leaving, with the radio
still telling the news.

Graham Greene said
happiness was hard.
I paraphrase and say that
we are most ourselves
when we are sad.

Cup after cup of hot water,
the bell ringing below me,
shaking the house about like a heart.

It's that time of the day
when everyone else thinks about home
and I write.

Poem for Anna

Hearing you read
in a sing-song voice
takes me here and there
like a kite.

Suddenly the roof
lifts off the auditorium
and your words fly out
into the afternoon,

random and unerring
as sky rockets

launched from your
golden head,

your thin yellow book,

your thin and steady hands.

The *mot juste*

His name was Matt
and he stood in front of me
in his Hawaiian print shirt
in the Westland High library,

and he told me he'd been reading
the dictionary because he was on the hunt
for new words like

monody.

He was doing a series of doors
pulled from junkyards
and backyards

(*monody monody*)

and these doors would carry words
other than
exit or *office manager*,
allowing a viewer to step
on through into a new linguistic world.

Step on fairly fast too,
not like walking through the pages
of a dictionary where the sleeve of your interest
is continually snagged by words like

monody monody monody.

He'd also tried reading the Bible,
he told me as he stood there with paint
on his hands, but this book had gone on
a bit and could have done with some editing.

Behind us the return slot
was thumping like a heartbeat
as people posted back their books.
They would go on then, to the bank
or through the revolving doors of a supermarket

or perhaps to a funeral
where they might also hear a monody

a *monody, melody or threnody*

and behind it the grey, the lamenting Tasman
loud in their ears.

For Joe, on a Monday afternoon

(for Joe Bennett)

You call to read me a column
on carrots and I decide:
you are an onion, you have many layers.
(It is Monday,
there is rain and a sun outside.)

Jenny Bornholdt said life
is a bowl of old onions:
it can make you both
laugh and weep.

I say – the taste of life
would be different without you,
less sharp, less sweet.

Love in a bookstore or your money back

I stood
in a bookstore
successfully picking up
poet after poet,

even Frank O'Hara
and T. S. Eliot, who had
always attracted me
most.

Their spines felt good
in my hands

and suddenly I realised:
this was a guarantee.

Love is always to be found
in bookstores.